<u>INDEX</u>

European Mudjahedins

In the summer of 2012, the first reports emerged of so-called "foreign fighters" (FF) leaving their country of origin or habitual residence to join the Syrian uprising against the Assad regime. Since then, the number of these "travellers" to the Syrian, and more recently, Iraqi battlefields has grown significantly: From September 2014 to September 2015 alone, the number of FF reportedly doubled and reached 30,000 combatants coming from 104 countries.

Some countries are directly affected by the FF issue by foiled or successful attacks, others by being transit countries or departing bases for non-national fighters. While the phenomenon of FF is not new, the sheer size and widespread origins has given the phenomenon a whole new dimension.

Experts and government officials have increasingly warned of the potential security threat this phenomenon might pose to Europe and beyond. Europol, for example, cautioned that FF returning from the battlefields could use "their training, combat experience, knowledge, and contacts" to carry out terrorist acts in the EU.4 Academic researchers and think tanks have confirmed this security threat, and also point out the psychological and social problems that returning FF might pose to themselves and their direct environments.

The past years have seen several attacks connected to FF. These include the January 2015 attacks on the headquarters of the satirical newspaper Charlie Hebdo, and the subsequent attack on a kosher supermarket in Paris, as well as an earlier attack by a French national, who had allegedly spent several months fighting in Syria before carrying out an assault on a Jewish museum in Brussels in May 2014.

But it was not until the tragic events that unfolded on the night of 13 November 2015 in the streets of Paris that fears of a large-scale attack involving groups of returnees from Syria/Iraq were painfully confirmed: At least seven of the perpetrators were alleged to have fought with the so-called "Islamic State" (IS). The most recent attacks in Brussels on 22 March 2016 only seem to underscore the deadly relevance of foreign fighters.

Austria

By September 2015, 230 identified individuals had left Austria for Syria/Iraq; 130 FF were still in the conflict zone and at least 34 had deceased. More recent open-source information points to estimates of up to 300 FF from Austria. According to the Austrian Ministry of Interior (MoI), the number of returnees may exceed 70 persons. In the course of a parliamentary inquiry conducted in March 2015, the MoI affirmed that seventeen women had left Austria as of 9 February 2015 for IS-controlled territory; some of whom were under eighteen at the time of their departure.

While the 2014 Annual Report for the Protection of the Constitution noted that the Austrian FF have no homogenous background, the US Country Reports on Terrorism (2014) point out that people departing from Austria were predominantly of Chechen, Turkish, and Balkan origin. Austrian news agencies further noted that most Austrian FF are second-generation immigrants of Chechen origin. The age range of FF is between 18 and 35 years.

According to the MoI, Austria is subject to a heightened but abstract danger from Islamist extremism and terrorism.7 Returnees are perceived as a potential threat. While the Ministry of Foreign Affairs (MFA) reported in response to the ICCT questionnaire that "there is no home-grown terrorism in Austria", the threat assessment provided by the MoI in its 2014 Annual Report on the Protection of the Constitution affirms that a home-grown terrorism scene has been developing since 2000.

The members are of heterogeneous ethnic background and their activities focus on recruitment and expansion of existing networks. This might mean that the threat perceived by the Austrian authorities – from domestic radicalisation and FF – is mainly connected to individuals with an immigration background, to non-nationals, or in fact, to returned FF. Indeed, the 2013 Annual Report on the Protection of the Constitution explicitly stated, for the first time, that returning FF represent a considerable threat to Austria, a notion confirmed by Austrian authorities in September 2015.

Austria does not have one, overall comprehensive CT strategy, but follows "a double-track approach of law enforcement and prevention", involving various government entities as well as civil society and academic institutions. The double-track approach pursued by Austria foresees the implementation of both judicial and security measures and of preventive measures. MFA officials state that a primary goal of Austrian policies is to engage with individuals in the early stages of the radicalization process in order to facilitate reintegration and strengthen resilience against extremist messages.

In December 2014, the Austrian government passed a series of acts, such as the Nationality Act, which states that dual nationals shall be stripped of their Austrian citizenship in case of voluntary participation in an armed group engaged in hostilities abroad. Similarly, the Passport Act prohibits the issuing, extension, and alteration of passports when facts lead to the assumption that the applicant might endanger public security as a member of a criminal organization.

These regulations also apply to identity cards. In July 2015, subsequent amendments were introduced through which the

Austrian Parliament "clarifi[ed] and tighten[ed] the reasons for exclusion of asylum status as well as for the refusal of issuing travel documents to recognized refugees and other legally residing non-nationals posing a threat to public security".

On the protection side, the Austrian Government has increased the budget of the national CT security authorities by up to €290 million until 2018, in particular for personnel, equipment, IT-security and forensic technology. In December 2014, the BVT also created a department for tracking and reporting radical content on the internet.

In addition, an amendment to the Border Controls Act aims at facilitating stricter checks of whether unaccompanied minors travel with their parents' consent. Furthermore, cross-border intelligence and police cooperation has been intensified, and border control has been strengthened. It has also taken "operative police measures [...] in order to prevent travels [sic] by potential Foreign Terrorist Fighters and to facilitate investigations for the prosecution of returnees".

Belgium

Most recent estimates from both official and non-government sources range between 420 to 516 individuals who have travelled to Syria/Iraq since 2011, making Belgium the EU MS with the highest number of FF per capita. An estimated 180–260 FF remain in the conflict zone; 60 to 70 have been killed, mostly in combat. Between 55–120 individuals had returned, and 50 tried to leave but were stopped (yet, these 50 are still included in some counts).

Regarding the profiles and composition of the Belgian FF contingent, Peter Van Ostaeyen provides detailed numbers in October 2015, indicating that 47 of the 516 are female, around 6% are converts, the age of 202 Belgian fighters varies between 14 and 69 (with an average of 25.7), that of the 266 individuals whose origin is known, most come from Brussels (101 of whom 24 from Molenbeek), Antwerp (72), Vilvoorde (28), and Mechelen (14); that 79 individuals can be linked to the group Sharia4Belgium which seems to have inspired many young Belgians to leave for the Levant; that at least five persons are fighting in pro-regime ranks, that at least 112 (but most likely more) are fighters/members of IS, and that around seventeen (but most likely many more) are fighting with Jabhat al-Nusra (JAN).

The motivation for leaving to fight abroad is very difficult to gauge. However, Prof. R. Coolsaet has offered a few preliminary observations: "They often mention earlier personal difficulties [...] that left them feeling stifled and ill at ease. Frequently, they express feelings of exclusion and absence of belonging, as if they didn't have a stake in society. For a significant number of them, drugs, petty crime and street violence have been part of their former life. From the sources mentioned, one gets the impression of solitary individuals, sometimes also estranged from family and friends, who at a certain point became angry as a result of their estrangement. Going to Syria is one of a number of possible outlets for their anger".

The Belgian government considers Belgium to be a potential target, since it is as member of the coalition against IS. Furthermore, it states that "Belgium has an open society, in the heart of Europe with a large number of FF going to and returning from Syria. The phenomenon of these FTF is considered a direct threat to our society". Furthermore, Belgium as a host country to major international institutions such as the EU and NATO, which can become a target themselves, runs an additional risk.

Bulgaria

According to the Bulgarian MoI, "[c]urrently there is no confirmed information regarding participation of Bulgarian nationals or foreigners staying in Bulgaria in terrorist activities of armed groups in Syria and Iraq". According to open-source information consulted by ICCT, up to ten Bulgarians are estimated to have travelled to Syria/Iraq.

Despite the lack of a confirmed number of FF from Bulgaria, the following anecdotal evidence suggests that Bulgaria is acting as a transit country for people from Europe and elsewhere willing to reach the conflict zones, or returning to their country of origin: In June 2014, for instance, a blacklisted, British IS fighter successfully crossed Bulgaria after six months in Syria, and was later arrested and sentenced in the UK. He admitted preparing for acts of terrorism, attending a camp, receiving training and possessing firearms. In December 2014, individuals from Brazil and Morocco were arrested at the Bulgarian-Turkish border, allegedly on their way to Syria. Bulgarian authorities also arrested a self-confessed associate of the perpetrators of the Charlie Hebdo attacks in Paris while he was on his way to Syria; he was then extradited to France.

In August 2015, there were reports of two IS fighters having entered Bulgaria through the Turkish border, allegedly a French national and a Romanian national. As a consequence, security at airports and train stations was heightened. In September 2015, a German citizen of Moroccan origin was extradited from Bulgaria to Germany suspected of IS affiliation and searched on the basis of a European Arrest Warrant. Lastly, in October 2015, three Dutch citizens were detained at the border and extradited for similar reasons (IS links and terrorism-related charges).

The MoI stated that, while the specific threat to the country remains moderate, a growing terrorist threat has been registered in Bulgaria since 1 January 2011 due to "the increased terrorist activity worldwide, the involvement of Bulgaria in the anti-terrorist coalition, the presence in the country of possible targets of attacks, and the hypothetical possibility of penetration of terrorist elements from abroad".

In line with assessing foreign terrorist elements and targets of those as a potential threat to the country, the only terrorist incident Bulgaria experienced in the studied timeframe was the 2012 Burgas bus suicide bombing, killing five Israeli tourists and one Bulgarian citizen while wounding 32 other Israeli citizens. Allegedly carried out by Hezbollah, the attack has no link to the foreign fighters (FF) phenomenon.

Furthermore, the MoI noted that "at the present moment, the level of radicalization of separate social groups in Bulgaria is assessed as low and, as a whole, the potentially vulnerable communities are relatively indifferent to the terrorist propaganda", so it is not possible to speak of the recruitment of Bulgarian FF as a phenomenon. However, MoI officials recognise the potential threat that returning FF may present in the short term, as a result of the dangerous skills they acquired on the battlefield, while in the long term, this threat may be exacerbated by the establishment of operational terrorist networks in the country by individuals who have European identification documents and may travel the country without restrictions.

Notwithstanding the lack of relevant pre-trial proceedings and legal cases initiated against FF, Bulgarian authorities raided some radical Muslim cells in cities with large Muslim minorities and Roma neighbourhoods in November 2014, where IS-linked propaganda material was found. Security forces searched more than 45 locations and carried out multiple arrests, including those of imams.

Cyprus

No information could be found on the number of FF from Cyprus, their profiles or backgrounds. In September 2014, police authorities in Cyprus investigated five people for possible facilitation of travel to conflict areas abroad, but no incriminating evidence was found. Nevertheless, there have been reports of Cyprus functioning as a transit country: At least a dozen British FF, and some Dutch FF were reported to have travelled to Syria/Iraq via Cyprus.

In April 2015, the threat level was raised from low to medium on a scale of five levels, as a result of the FF phenomenon, the country's proximity to the conflict zones as well as the number and seriousness of terrorist attacks that occurred in Europe throughout 2015.

The only terrorism-related incidents experienced by Cyprus were linked to the Lebanese group Hezbollah. In July 2012, a Swedish national of Lebanese origin was arrested and sentenced to a four-and-a-half year prison term for plotting an attack on Israeli targets in Cyprus. The second incident occurred in May 2015 when a Lebanese national with a Canadian passport was arrested in Cyprus. A huge amount of ammonium nitrate was discovered in his house. The following month, he was sentenced to six years of imprisonment for "participating in, aiding and abetting a terrorist organization (Hezbollah)".

Denmark

According to the Danish Security and Intelligence Service (PET), at least 125 people have left Denmark to travel to Syria/Iraq since January 2011, with a quarter deemed to still be in the conflict zone. At least 27 have died abroad, some while committing suicide attacks. While the majority of the Danish contingent joined IS, PET estimates that "a small number, including Kurds and Shiites, has gone to the conflict zone in Syria and Iraq to fight militant Islamist groups or other armed opposition groups".

With regards to the characteristics of the FF originating in Denmark, PET affirms that the majority are Danish citizens, but with very diverse ethnic origins, including ethnic Danes. Ministry of Justice (MoJ) officials note that "the individuals that leave Denmark to join IS are mainly young Sunni Muslim", including "a number of converts". Women are estimated to constitute 10% of all those who went to Syria. In its 2013 threat assessment report, PET warned that "the group that has left for Syria is younger and more varied than those who left for Afghanistan, Iraq, and Somalia".

PET assesses that the individuals who have left Denmark are mainly affiliated with Islamist circles in cities such as Copenhagen, Aarhus, and Odense and half of the returnees are part of Islamist circles. Public sources point to the fact that at least 22 FF came from the port city of Aarhus and attended the Grimhojvej mosque, which has refused to denounce IS. Lastly, PET assesses that just under half of the individuals who have left Denmark for the conflict zone have been involved in crime.

With respect to the motivations of those willing to leave and join armed groups in the conflict zone, PET points to a wide range: "Some wish to help their fellow Muslims in Syria and do humanitarian work. Others wish to fight the Assad regime. For some the establishment of an Islamic State in Syria is a priority and they may be motivated by achieving what they regard as martyrdom. Finally, maybe there are some who go to Syria in search of excitement and adventure".

With regards to FF, PET provided a broad assessment of the threat to Denmark: "The threat mainly emanates from individuals and small groups with a militant Islamist outlook. Propaganda from militant groups in Iraq and Syria contributes to the radicalisation of individuals and circles in Denmark and to individuals travelling abroad to join these groups.

Moreover, individuals who are influenced by militant Islamist propaganda and at the same time are linked to criminal circles with a high degree of proneness to violence may become increasingly significant to the terror threat. Returnees from the conflict in Syria and Iraq pose a particular terror threat to Denmark because of the skills they might have acquired. A capacity to conduct terrorist attacks, which can be carried out after short planning, using easily accessible weapons, is present in Denmark".

France

It is estimated that more than 900 individuals had left France for Syria/Iraq by October 2015. Overall, the number of radicalised French nationals or residents involved in jihadist networks, but not necessarily having travelled to Syria/Iraq, is estimated to be close to 2,000.

By November 2015, an estimated 570 FF were still in the conflict zone, of whom close to 200 were female; about 140 had died (including approximately ten in suicide attacks), and 246 had returned. In addition, it is estimated that 85 minors are involved in jihadist networks and ten are in Syria/Iraq. Regarding affiliation, it is estimated that about 75% had joined IS and 25% JAN.

As with other countries, there is no typical profile of a French FF. FF are known to come from all regions and socio-economic environments. While many French FF are young men with a pre-existing criminal record, there is also a growing contingent of women and even entire families who aim to settle permanently in the Caliphate. Converts represent 23% of the French FF contingent.

France's national terrorist threat system, the Vigipirate Plan, has two levels and one sub-level (vigilance, reinforced vigilance, and attack alert). The response to the ICCT questionnaire – which was returned prior to the Paris attacks – stated that the main threat to France was home-grown terrorism and the phenomenon of FF as a whole. The Paris area has been on the highest level since the January 2015 attacks, with the level throughout the country being raised to the same level following the November 2015 events.

Germany

The German security authorities recently published a new study that brings together information on 677 individuals who departed Germany for Syria or Iraq before June 30, 2015.

According to the German authorities, more than 800 people have left Germany for Syria or Iraq since the beginning of the Syrian conflict, though it is not possible to verify that they all reached the region. Around one third of the departees is known or assumed to have returned to Germany, of whom 70 are thought to have experienced armed combat with Islamic State, or at least undergone military training. About 130 Islamists from Germany are presumed to have been killed in the conflict.

Significant numbers of people began travelling to Syria or Iraq in 2012/2013. A first peak happened in the third quarter of 2013. Although numbers declined in the subsequent months, they peaked again in the second quarter of 2014 and remained relatively high during the rest of the year. At the same time, the number of departures dropped significantly in 2015, with only some 20+ in each of the first two quarters.

The departees are 79% male and 21% female. However, the share of female departees rose significantly after the proclamation of the Caliphate by the Islamic State on June 29, 2014, from just 15% pre-proclamation and an astonishing 38 % post-proclamation.

The age range is 15 to 62 years, with an arithmetic mean of 25.9 years. The largest group (188 individuals) belongs to the age bracket 22-25 years, while 139 were aged 18-21 years and 124 were aged 26-29 years. Again, there are significant differences between the groups who departed prior and after the proclamation of the Caliphate (coined 'early departees' and 'late departees', respectively): the mean age of the late departees is three years younger than the early departees (23.7 vs. 26.6 years); and the percentage of minors (i.e. individuals under the age of 18 years) is considerably higher (12% vs. 5%).

Of the 628 individuals with known marital status, 34% were single, 25% legally married and 32% married under Islamic law. 267 departees are known to have children. 60% of the 548 individuals with known living conditions owned a home prior to their departure. Close to 90% of all departees lived in urban areas.

61% of the departees were born in Germany, with a broad range of other places of birth, the most significant of which are Turkey (6%), Syria (5%), the Russian Federation (5%), and Afghanistan (3%). Including the individuals born in Germany, a total of 82.4% of all departees belonged to migrant families. With regard to this variable, there are no differences between the pre- and post-Caliphate phase.

63 departees are known to have attended a school at the point of their departure. 115 individuals are known to have begun a vocational training. Of these, 49% had completed this training prior to their departure, 31% had dropped out before, and 20% were still in training when they left Germany. 81 persons are known to have begun university studies, of which 14% had completed university, 28% had discontinued it, and 59% were still enrolled at the time of their departure. Another 94 individuals are known to have had a regular job at that point, while 147 others were unemployed.

At least 116 departees are converts. At least 547 individuals are considered to belong to the Salafi spectrum, while only 22 are known not have belonged to this religious current.

68% had contacts to supra-regional Salafists/Islamists and/or Salafi groups, including both smaller local formations and long-distance contacts. Five especially relevant groups were identified that contributed 10 to 19 departees each.

Two thirds of the departees have been the subject of criminal investigations. 225 individuals were suspected of or tried for criminal offences prior to their Islamist radicalisation, with violent attacks (assault, robbery, etc.) and property crime accounting for 29 % each, followed by drug trafficking (16 %). Politically motivated offences played no significant role.

After their radicalisation had begun, 264 individuals were suspected of or tried for criminal offences. Politically motivated offences (under German law) now accounted for nearly a third of these (31%), followed by violent attacks (24%) and property crime (20%). Drug-related offences dropped to just 4% of the total. Of the individuals with a criminal record, more than half (53%) were suspected of or tried for three or more offences, and nearly a third (32%) were suspected of or tried for six or more crimes.

The vast majority of departees were radicalised in "real life environments". In most cases the internet played no major role, and only a few individuals were purely radicalised online.

With regard to the most important contributing factors, of the 514 departees whose respective radicalization processes are known, 81% had contacts to extreme Salafi groups, which highlights the relevance of this orientation. Close social contacts with extremist views were assessed as relevant factors in 96% of the cases investigated.

In many cases the radicalization process was very quick. Nearly half (48%) of all departees appeared to depart Germany within one year of the radicalization process beginning, with close to a quarter (23%) departing within six months of the start of this process. 68% of the departees left within two years.

The tendency towards short radicalization processes among supporters of Islamic State appears to have accelerated following the proclamation of the so-called Caliphate. The median duration of the radicalization process dropped from 27 to 20 months, and correspondingly, the share of departees who left Germany within one year after the beginning of their radicalization climbed from 42% to 60% in the post-Caliphate phase.

Regarding the profile of FF, 40% hold only German citizenship, 20% hold dual nationality (German and another), and 40% left from Germany but are not German citizens. The female proportion stands at 20%. Five percent were under the age of eighteen when they left and the majority of those who have left are younger than 30 years of age. Twelve percent are believed to be converts to Islam. Most of those traveling come from North Rhine-Westphalia and Hesse, though a "large number of travelers also come[s] from Berlin, Bavaria and Hamburg". Additionally, many German FF are believed to have either been unemployed or in the low-paid/skilled employment sector prior to departure. Two-thirds were known to the police prior to departure.

Regarding possible motives for FF to travel abroad, the German MFA, while referring to a 2014 study on 378 radicalization cases, noted "the interest of FF to live in a true Islamic area and to fight for this or other Islamist goals or otherwise support the Islamist cause". The study also noted the relative speed with which individuals radicalize, often in less than 12 months.

Spain

The Spanish MoI reported in November 2015 that 139 FF had left Spain, and 25 individuals had returned. According to a report published in the same month by Fernando Reinares and Carola Garcia Calvo, there are an estimated 120 Spain-linked FF. Ten percent of those who went to Syria from Spain were female.

Reinares and Calvo183 also reconstructed the profiles of twenty Spanish residents that had travelled to fight with jihadist groups in

Syria before 2014. Eleven of the twenty are Spanish citizens, while the remaining nine are Moroccan nationals living in Spain; most lived in the Spanish enclave Ceuta in North Africa, but also in Girona and Malaga. The majority are between their mid 20s and early 30s; they were mostly married and with children; and were low-skilled, (un)employed workers as well as students at the time of their departure. Several were already known to the police (especially in Ceuta) and implicated in drug trafficking. Out of the 20, at least three young Muslim Spanish nationals residing in Ceuta became suicide bombers.

UK

According to the UK Office for Security and Counter-Terrorism (OSCT), approximately 700 individuals had left for Syria/Iraq since January 2011, of whom 315 are currently in the conflict area, over half returned, and approximately 70 died. The total number is below the latest TSG estimate which indicates 760 FF as an official count in November 2015. The OSCT further reported that the majority of UK FF have joined IS, and that a majority holds British citizenship.

Most FF are between 18 and 30 years of age, although the average age is reducing. Almost all are Muslim. The OSCT stated that it is not possible to deduce one unifying motivation for all FF, and that multiple underlying factors play a role, mostly related to a weak social status that makes individuals vulnerable to IS' message(s), including through the Internet and social media. Yet, in 2013, Maher concluded that "many of those travelling to Syria as foreign fighters are male; in their twenties, of South-Asian ethnic origin, with recent connections to higher education, and with links to individuals or groups who have international connections".

Since April 2010, more than 800 people have been arrested for terrorism-related offences in the UK. Of these more than 200 have been charged and over 140 have been successfully prosecuted. Of the 721 persons charged with terrorism-related offences between 11 September 2001 and 31 December 2014, 452 have been convicted. In the year ending 31 December 2014 there were 289 persons arrested for terrorism related offences, an increase of 30% compared with the 223 arrests the previous year. There were 111 charges following terrorism-related arrests. Of these, 96 (86%) were for terrorism-related offences, an increase from the 56% in the previous year.

As of October 2014, 29 of the 77 persons charged with terrorism-related offences had been proceeded against. Of these, 26 persons were convicted of an offence [...] Of the 96 persons charged with a terrorism-related offence in the year ending 31 December 2014, 33 were prosecuted, 30 of whom were convicted. A further 55 cases were awaiting prosecution proceedings to commence [...]. There have been many terrorism cases in the UK, some of which have included individuals who have travelled to Syria to engage in terrorist activity. People who commit, plan and support acts of terror abroad and seek to return to the UK will be prosecuted by the UK authorities.

Whether a prosecution for an offence is justified in an individual case is a matter for the Crown Prosecution Service to decide after a full police investigation [...]. The most common offence for which persons have been charged with under terrorism legislation since 11 September 2001 is 'preparation for terrorist acts' (section 5 of TACT 2006), which has accounted for 14% of all terrorism-related charges since then, and 31% in the year ending 31 December 2014. Further details of the legislation under which persons have been charged following a terrorism-related arrest can be found in the attached table".

Italy

According to the Italian MoI, 87 FF departed from Italy between 1 January 2011 and late October 2015. Fifty-seven are allegedly in the conflict zone and eighteen have died. The response of the government also indicated that fifteen FF had joined IS, two had joined JAN, and seven had joined other opposition forces including the FSA.224 The Italian Defence Minister noted that only twelve FF had Italian passports, with six also holding another (dual) nationality.

Holland

According to the National Coordinator for Security and Counterterrorism (NCTV), by 1 November 2015, around 220 individuals had left the Netherlands "for jihadist purposes", with 40 returnees, 42 deceased and 140 remaining in Syria/Iraq.288 Most of those killed were members of IS, and all of them male, resulting in a proportionate increase in the percentage of females within the whole FF contingent.

Publicly available information about the background of Dutch FF is scarce. Some initial research289 indicates that the majority are male and under the age of 25. The majority have lower or lower-middle class socio-economic backgrounds, low to medium levels of education and limited chances on the labour market. Dutch FF were raised in both traditional religious immigrant (Moroccan, Somali, Antillean, Turkish) and Islamic families, as well as in ethnically Dutch settings.

Many have been exposed to crime and drug abuse (in their immediate social circle); some have had a traumatic experience in their life in the period prior to travelling to Syria/Iraq. Some are deeply frustrated about their own societal position or that of their ethnic group, feeling that they did not have a future in the Netherlands or any way to improve their position. There is a notable cluster of Dutch FF stemming from The Hague, but also other towns, such as Delft, Zoetermeer, Gouda, and Arnhem.

A final point of interest is that mental health conditions may also play a role among the group of (potential) Dutch FF. In a study among 140 (potential) FF, whose files were cross-referenced with police databases, it appeared that "individuals with histories of behavioral problems and disorders are over-represented". The Netherlands uses a four level threat analysis scale: Minimal, limited, substantial and critical. The threat level at the time of writing was "substantial" (level 3), which means that the chance of an attack is real, though there are no specific indications of an imminent terrorist attack.

The threat is predominantly jihadist in nature. It remains complex and involves a variety of actors. In addition to international and local networks that pose a threat, the threat comes also from lone actor terrorists. The Paris attacks, which occurred four days after the last official threat assessment was issued, did not lead to a higher threat level in the Netherlands.

Poland

Between 20 to 40 Polish nationals are believed to have travelled to Syria/Iraq, most of them residing at the time of departure not in Poland itself but in other European countries. News reports have shed light on the profiles of three Polish FF, each also holding German nationality and residing in Germany prior to departure. One man was allegedly killed in northern Iraq in February 2015 while fighting for IS. His sister was prosecuted and sentenced by a German court for providing support to IS in the form of money and video equipment.

She is said to have travelled to Syria in 2013, and was reportedly "radicalized while she was still at secondary school in Bonn". Finally, a man allegedly carried out a suicide attack on a refinery in Iraq in June 2015, together with 3 other FF. Poland has a terrorism threat scale with four levels, as well as a "zero" level. The current terrorism threat level in Poland is assessed as low ("zero").

Poland's National Counter-Terrorism Program states that, although there is a high threat of terrorist attacks in the world, the risk in Poland remains relatively low. The country is seen only as a "backup" target, by "persons or organizations who come from so called high-risk countries or countries which are politically unstable". Although the threat posed by individuals who radicalized through the internet or contact with extremist circles is acknowledged as real, the risk of home-grown radicalization is perceived as relatively low compared to other European countries.

Portugal

It is estimated that about a dozen Portuguese nationals or residents have left for Syria/Iraq since January 2011, five of which have reportedly died: Two in a US air strike in Kobane, one while committing a suicide attack against an Iraqi military post, and a father and son who died in combat. Reportedly, the majority had converted to Islam within a few years to months before traveling to the conflict zone. Many have origins in former Portuguese colonies or have long lived abroad. Some resided in other European countries (France, Luxembourg, the Netherlands, the UK) for longer than they had lived in Portugal, and many also hold dual nationalities from other European countries. Five of them are known to have lived and met in Leyton, London. One is identified as a Portuguese-Dutch woman who resided in the Netherlands and left to Syria to marry a Portuguese FF.

Portugal perceives the threat of terrorism and FF lower than other European countries. One foiled terrorist attack was reported in news reports: in July 2014, a Dutch national of Angolese origins was arrested at the Lisbon airport after boarding an airplane with a 21 cm blade. He had previously trained in Syria and has been charged by a Portuguese court for attempting to carry out a terrorist attack.

Basic Characteristics of FF

Although there is not one typical profile of a European FF, some key characteristics can be identified. Based on this research, FF today are mostly young men between the ages of eighteen and mid-to-late twenties, with some countries reporting that between 4% and 10% of FF are under eighteen,263 whereas in four countries in Eastern and Southern Europe, the FF contingent is older, with more than 50% being over 30. The proportion of females in the total FF contingent varies between 6% and 30%, with some countries indicating that the number has grown in recent months.

Little data could be found on the marital status of all (i.e. male and female) departed FF. However, information from five countries indicates that around half are married, whereas one Southern European country had a majority of unmarried FF.

On the basis of the data available for nine countries accounting for over 30% of the total contingent, most FF originate from large metropolitan areas or peripheral suburbs. The majority of German FF come from cities, for instance from Berlin and Hamburg. It is notable that many FF originate from the same urban neighbourhood.

This is the case for example in Aarhus, Copenhagen, and Odense in Denmark, as well as Gothenburg in Sweden, and Brussels or Antwerp in Belgium, or Delft, Zoetermeer, Arnhem, and The Hague in the Netherlands. This seems to indicate that there are already-existing (extremist) networks in these areas, that a circle of friends radicalizes as a group and decides to leave together, or recruits those friends remaining at home while already in the conflict zones.

The number of converts to Islam among FF is significant. In the case of two Eastern European countries, this percentage reaches 100% (note, however, that the total number of FF in each of these countries is below five). For MS with higher numbers of FF, the research illustrates that between 6% and 23% of FF are converts; 12% in the case of the German FF contingent. Another example of the importance of converts is the composition of a group behind a foiled terrorist attack in Barcelona in June 2015, where five out of the eleven captured IS sympathizers had converted to Islam from either atheism or Christianity.

Other data was less conclusive. For example, there is a significant variation when it comes to the national background of deportees. In two Western European countries, the majority hold a nationality other than the one of the country where they departed from; whereas in another Western European country the inverse trend can be observed, with the majority of FF holding at least the citizenship of the country of departure (or dual nationality).

In certain cases, strong links to previous criminal activities were found, for instance, in the case of France, Austria, and Slovenia. While, for two countries, none of the FF had a prior criminal record, for five others, between 24% and a "majority" had been convicted for criminal offenses. It should also be noted that in some EU countries, persons who left for Syria/Iraq were linked to pre-existing Islamist circles back home.

For instance, in the case of Denmark, some FF "are affiliated with known Islamist circles [...] in Copenhagen and other major cities". In the case of Luxembourg, all those who left had previous links to Islamist networks. In one Northern European country, the percentage of those linked to Islamist circles reached 85%. Lastly, ICCT also aimed to find out whether FF (have) had mental-health problems. From the data provided by only three MS, between 0 and up to 20% of FF fall within this category.

From Activism to Violent Action

The Wide-Range of Motivations of Foreign Fighters Based on the information collected through the ICCT questionnaire, FF motivations to depart include a wide variety of push and pull factors: Solidarity with other "fellow Muslims" abroad (in Syria mostly, and especially during the early stages of FF travel), the fight against the Alawite Assad regime in Syria, the desire to live in a territory ruled by Islamic law, alienation and social exclusion felt in Europe, as well as the desire to conduct jihad. For some, the search for excitement and adventure play a role, as does peer pressure and the prospects of life in the caliphate, such as marriage and housing. At least one response to the ICCT questionnaire mentioned the relative ease of travel to Syria/Iraq by land as a motivating/facilitating factor to undertake the journey to the conflict zone.

Other sources indicate that FF' motives could also relate to more politically-oriented factors, such as EU MS' foreign policy (past or current military engagement against armed groups close or affiliated to IS or al Qaeda) or EU national integration policies allegedly alienating Muslim groups.

Both the data gathered for this study and academic literature emphasize a new generation of foreign combatants, different from the Afghan "Holy warriors" and "hardened jihadists", "galvanized by hateful religious and political ideologies [... and] determined to turn the global tide against the 'infidel' regimes".

The three previous generations of FF show differences with this generation in terms of socio-economic and educational background, battlefield experience, age range and motivational factors. This so-called fourth generation of FF, can, according to Coolsaet,271 be split up in two main groups: The first group builds on pre-existing social relations and their travel is "another form of deviant behavior, next to membership of street gangs, rioting, drug trafficking and juvenile delinquency". Joining IS then offers a "thrilling, larger-than-life dimension to their way of life". The second group, however, showed no previous deviant behavior, or specific distinction from their peers.

Key features of this group is the absence of a future and feelings of exclusion, and their "search for belonging and a cause to embrace". This difference is largely related to the different role religion seems to play as a motivational factor for EU FF compared to previous generations.

Contrary to previous waves of FF who departed for Afghanistan, Iraq, or Somalia, today's cohort appears to be younger and less educated in Islam and, in the words of Oliver Roy, "more radicals than Islamists". As pointed out in a recent paper, most young Sunni Muslims became susceptible to fundamentalist interpretations of militant Islam after they found it difficult to integrate into European societies due to cultural, religious and social differences.

The psychology literature on the FF phenomenon confirms this assessment: "The perception of grievance drives the search for a violence-justifying ideology, not the other way around".

The language of jihad then only legitimates the grievance, offering a designated culprit and a direct justification to fight the wrong, whether that is poor integration, real or perceived marginalization, relative deprivation, or discrimination. As such, the decision to make hijra "to the land of Islam" may be less of a religious obligation than an emotional response to a feeling of injustice in their home societies, or what French novelist Erick Orsenna calls "the breeding ground of hopelessness" following the Charlie Hebdo attacks.

Although much is still unknown about the underlying grievances of radicalization and the trigger that pushes people over the edge to the extent that they support the violent cause of organizations such as IS or JAN, it is important to stress that evidence so far does not seem to support the notion that religious conviction is the initial push factor in most cases, even though it does play a role as a pull factor exploited by recruiters, and as a legitimation of the violence later on in the process of radicalization.

Patterns of Radicalization

This research, through questionnaires and open-source material, disclosed a wide variety of radicalization patterns with radicalization taking place in various environments, such as within the family, within friendship groups, and in mosque or prison communities. In a study on AQI, it was indicated that FF overwhelmingly joined the jihad via sympathizers networks (33.5%) and personal social networks (29%). The role of social media was also noted as significant in several responses to the ICCT questionnaire. With approximately 46,000 Twitter accounts operating on behalf of IS, social media represents a powerful instrument in IS propaganda. Online extremism expert J. M. Berger notes that "many, perhaps most, potential recruits first learn about ISIS from the media, only then seeking it out on social media".

The radicalization process appears to be the result of a combination of individual and context-related factors. Notwithstanding the heterogeneity of EU FF' backgrounds, various analyses and reports emphasize socially vulnerable profiles, mainly composed of marginalized and single individual or cliques, youth in transitional stages of their lives, who discreetly radicalize, "under the radar", and in a relatively short period of time. The youngest perpetrator of the Paris attacks, for instance, allegedly went from smoking and using drugs to radicalization and leaving for Syria in just one month. German authorities also emphasize this new tendency of accelerated radicalization, with many FF radicalizing in a matter of months.

Based on the data acquired through the ICCT questionnaires, once radicalized in Europe, the vast majority of European FF joined IS in Syria/Iraq. Very few joined JAN or other opposition forces. This concurs with a 2014 ICSR report, stating that IS is "very willing" to take in FF, even those who do not speak Arabic or those who did not receive any specific military training, whereas JAN is more reluctant to integrate unknown recruits.

Even though EU MS are not all equally affected by FF, all countries generally perceive the FF phenomenon as posing a serious threat to society, either in the form of further radicalization of home-grown networks or the potential of terror attacks involving returnees. As pointed out by Barak Mendelsohn, EU FF "are regarded by IS as more beneficial when used outside the arena, mostly for terrorist attacks in their home countries. These fighters are especially valued for their ability to travel and enter Western countries with relative ease". Even countries which have not (yet) experienced any problems are aware that the FF phenomenon represents a potential threat.

Europe has witnessed tragic incidents recently, triggering an increase in threat levels, enhanced security measures, and even, in the aftermath of the 13 November 2015 Paris attacks, to the French government declaring a state of emergency. The majority of MS consider the FF phenomenon as a serious threat to their national societies. Fourteen MS make use of threat level assessment mechanism. Only five of these assess the threat level in their country to be low or below average. Eleven MS have increased their threat levels since 2011, when the Syrian conflict commenced and the issue of FF became more pertinent.

Incidents such as those in Paris also typically led to proposals for new policies, laws and measures, ranging from more resources for the security apparatus, to the tracking and if possible, closing down of websites, the enactment of new criminal law provisions, and criminalizing conduct for offenses committed abroad (extra-territorial jurisdiction) and public apology of terrorism.

In a 2014 study that did not specifically address the Syria/Iraq cases, it was stated that only one out of every fifteen or twenty returnees might be interested in terrorist activities in their home countries. The situation might be different with the IS-affiliated FF, especially because the blowback case varies enormously between conflicts, so we cannot extrapolate averages to individual conflicts like Syria.

Since few of the FF are arrested upon return and a sizeable number are still abroad or have died in the course of terrorist and CT operations, it is difficult to understand the motivations behind their return. One study by the Dutch Security and Intelligence Service (AIVD) offered various different reasons for returning: being disillusioned, being traumatized, (feelings of) betrayal, realization of the atrocities, and regret, as well as having plans to recruit others or commit attacks in their countries of departure. The latter category – upon return to their country of departure – will put them in the position to import their violent ideology and techniques.

Sweden

It is estimated that about 300 Swedish nationals or residents have travelled to Syria/Iraq. A sizeable portion appears to come from the area of Gothenburg.380 In recent years, Sweden has witnessed an increase in the number of FF.

In their 2014 annual report, Swedish Security Service (SÄPO) noted that, "[f]or several years, there was [a] limited number of individuals travelling from Sweden to engage in armed combat in other countries, whereas today we know that hundreds of individuals have left Sweden to join ISIL. This trend shows no signs of slowing down". According to statements by SÄPO head Anders Thornberg, up to 250 to 300 Swedes have travelled to Syria/Iraq in the past three years. About 125 are still there, of which 90 are men and 35 are women. About 40 were killed while in Syria/Iraq.384 It has been reported that affiliation to either IS or Al-Nusra sometimes depends on when and with whom a FF crosses the border.

The area of Gothenburg appears particularly affected: an integration police officer said that it has one of the highest numbers of IS FF per capita in Europe. Angered, a poor suburb of Gothenburg, has reportedly "become a recruitment hub for jihadist departing from Sweden".

A news essay provides the following numbers and profiles: "According to local authorities, as of November 2014 there were at least 50 fighters from Gothenburg who had traveled to Syria and Iraq, with 22 of them still in the conflict zone. Of the Gothenburg fighters, 11 were women. At least 18 had returned. In all of Sweden, at least 80 fighters have returned, with some traveling back to Syria again. There are unconfirmed estimates from former foreign fighters that there may be as many as 150 fighters from Gothenburg alone."

On radicalization, the essay noted: "Recruitment into extremist milieus often occurs quietly in apartments or at night in small gatherings in select mosques. In certain parts of Angered, there are "garage mosques," or unofficial places of worship, which make little or no effort to conceal their activities".

Sweden has a formal terrorist threat scale with five levels, but it is aimed at a limited number of stakeholders and not the general public. This is because "assessments of the terrorist threat to Sweden and Swedish interests are based on secret information, and therefore the assessments themselves are also classified as secret".

Al Maqdisi

It is news to few observers that thousands, even millions, of young Muslims are influenced—to some extent—by jihadi literature circulating on various Islamist websites and discussion forums. The mujahideen's use of the internet for communication, indoctrination, recruitment and public relations has been well demonstrated. Through this medium, a field of preachers and ideologues compete for the vast audience of young Muslims, attempting to sway their opinion and bring them to the "correct" practice and understanding of Islam. Those backing the global jihadi movement have succeeded in capturing this audience—perhaps more so than other contenders—and have gained a wide following of careful but loyal readers.

The literature is critical because it provides deeper motivation to the believer, who seeks ideological backing before taking action. A group of Muslim scholars—Abu Muhammad al-Maqdisi, Abu Basir al-Tartusi, Abu Qatada al-Filistini, 'Abd al-Qadir bin 'Abd al-'Aziz and a few other Saudi clerics—are the primary Salafi opinion-makers guiding the jihadi movement. These scholars are relied upon for their credibility since they have either been imprisoned or exiled by their home countries. They are also perceived as being true to Islam and putting the interests of Muslims before themselves, making them sincere, legitimate and incorruptible. For the mujahideen, they are portrayed as scholarly authorities and the source for doctrinal legitimacy.

Surprisingly, al-Qaeda leaders Osama bin Laden and Ayman al-Zawahiri are not highly cited in jihadi literature. They are not considered authorities in Islamic law or looked to as the ideological force behind the jihadi movement. Indeed, in the world of Salafi-Jihadi ideology, they are relatively minor players. One possible reason for this is that the two are figureheads, pioneers in carrying out successful attacks against one of the enemies of Muslims. This suggests that there is a role for charismatic leaders to bring Muslims to jihad, as soldiers to the battlefield, but there is a separate role for these Salafi scholars in setting the broader goals for the movement, the limits and terms of engagement and selecting valid and legal targets. They are, in essence, creating the Islamic legal framework for this struggle so that the basis upon which it is waged will be sound. It is then left to strategists and mujahid leaders to conduct successful campaigns within this framework.

There is no single governing body for determining Islamic law in the Muslim world. Movements tend to center around persuasive and influential scholars that can grant them legitimacy in the eyes of other Muslims. This has been the case for the Salafi movement, including militant Salafis who form the global jihadi movement. Although the mujahideen are not held accountable to their constituency, they understand the need for their fellow Muslims to support their actions, provide them with funding and safe haven and ultimately be able to mobilize them when needed. Accordingly, the advice and writings of Salafi scholars carry much weight with the mujahideen and Muslim readers—regardless of their affiliation.

For the most influential scholars of the Salafi movement, such as Abu Muhammad al-Maqdisi, Abu Qatada and Abu Basir, the end goal is never jihad itself. The objective is to bring Muslims to a Salafi reading of Islam and then to deliver salvation to the global Muslim community. As such, the primary element of the literature is the meaning and implementation of the Sharia. The scholars first bring their interpretation of Islamic law on various political and social issues and present their advice on the appropriate action. The common ground among the scholars behind the jihadi movement is their rejection of Muslims living under apostate laws and political systems governing outside what God has decreed. The required response—for all, but to differing degrees and with differing tactics—is resistance.

This drive to instill Islamic law into Muslim society, and ultimately recreate that society under their interpretation of the law, often translates into an endorsement for violent jihad as practiced by bin Laden and others. While there are many Muslim scholars who call for these sources of law to be the primary factors in how Muslims live, the important distinction lies in how one should confront political systems that rule by law other than Sharia. The debate over law and society is critical in jihadi literature. It establishes the framework through which young Muslims should struggle; for these scholars, it is clear their aim is not jihad, but the creation of such a society through jihad, an obligatory struggle for the believer.

Biography

Asim Tahir al-Barqawi, better known as Abu Muhammad al-Maqdisi, is one of the most prolific contemporary jihadi ideologues and a classically trained scholar. He was born in Nablus in 1959, but has been imprisoned intermittently since the 1990s by the Jordanian authorities for his criticism of the government and calls for jihad. Al-Maqdisi is regarded as one of the highest living authorities in Islam for Salafis, jihadis and other conservative Sunni Muslims who share elements of his program. His imprisonment, however, seems to have had little effect on his scholarly output. He was the most frequently cited living Salafi scholar, indicating the wide range of jihadis (from strategists to mujahideen to fellow scholars) that cite his writings.

Al-Maqdisi is well traveled; he moved to Kuwait as a child and later undertook studies in the University of Mosul in Iraq. After that al-Maqdisi traveled through Saudi Arabia, Pakistan and Afghanistan, where he met various jihadi groups and wrote some of his most famous books, such as Millat 'Ibrahim wa da'awet al-anbiya wa'l murseleen (The Creed of Abraham and the Preaching of the Prophets and the Deliverers) and Al-kawashif al-jaliyya fi kufr al-dawla al-Sa'udiyya (The Shameful Actions Manifest in the Saudi State's Disbelief).

In 1992 al-Maqdisi returned to Jordan and started to preach his ideology, which quickly spread among some youngsters. The shaykh criticized Jordanian officials, denouncing their rule as illegitimate and opposed to the Shari`a. A combination of direct rhetoric and well-circulated stories of how he confronted the judges and his interrogators by calling them tyrants and disbelievers, soon established al-Maqdisi as a charismatic ideologue and leader of Salafi-Jiahdism.

Al-Maqdisi's texts are frequently aimed at the youth in Jordanian prisons and similar Muslims around the world that are encouraged to hold steadfast to the path of jihad in accordance with the principles of Islamic law detailed in his texts. To be sure, the legal arguments are lost on many of his students who lack formal Islamic legal training, but he provides contemporary examples to buttress his points.

Many of his texts are in response to criticisms of jihad by other Salafi clerics, typically from the Gulf states or Saudi Arabia. Other writings include the education of the next generation of leaders, numerous issues relating to resistance to tyrannical regimes and the need to uphold the Sharia and one of his most-widely read works, the Creed of Abraham, on monotheistic faiths (which is highly critical of contemporary Christians and Jews).

Through his writings, al-Maqdisi sets out the "correct" agenda for the various mujahideen groups to follow, what their intentions and objectives should be as they enter jihad, what preparation is required and what they should avoid (such as hasty actions that make the mujahideen look inept, inexperienced, or indifferent to killing innocent Muslims). There are more nuanced discussions of espionage, defining apostasy, takfir (labeling another Muslim an unbeliever), different examples of interaction with tyrannical rule and explanations of when resistance is obligatory for the believer.

Yet, in the end, a clear direction is set out for the mujahideen and those who support their cause on how best to proceed.

Al-Maqdisi's calls for unity are respected because of the scholarly weight behind his name and reputation. This also exposes one of the movement's weaknesses, and the shortcomings of governments confronting jihadi ideologues: a blow to his standing or a publicly lost debate would likely do much more to damage the unity of the jihadi movement than would his imprisonment.

On March 12, 2008 Abu Muhammad al-Maqdisi—born Isam Muhammad Tahir al-Barqawi in 1959—was released from a Jordanian prison after almost three years imprisonment without trial. Maqdisi has long played a pivotal role in defining jihadist ideology. After taking part in the Afghan jihad of the 1980s, he refined the ideology of declaring takfir against other Muslims—i.e. defining them as apostates and thus deserving of death—leading to the creation of jihadist groups in Jordan and 1995 attacks in Saudi Arabia—whose government he had denounced as un-Islamic as early as 1989. Between 1995 and 1999, Maqdisi was imprisoned in Jordan, during which time he expanded his ideas and built new radical networks with the help of his right-hand man, Abu Musab al-Zarqawi. From 1999, Maqdisi has spent most of his time in Jordanian prisons, reemerging briefly in 2005 before being re-imprisoned for giving an interview to al-Jazeera television in which he criticized Zarqawi's attacks on civilians while reiterating his support for a broader jihad against the West and "un-Islamic" governments. Despite his long prison terms, however, Maqdisi has written and distributed several accessible books addressing key issues such as democracy, takfir and jihadist tactics, giving him an almost unmatched influence over the evolution of jihadist theory.

Maqdisi's Influence

Maqdisi's latest release from prison—apparently on grounds of ill-health—was reported extensively on radical Islamic websites. Significantly, even Islamic extremists outside the Arab world reacted euphorically to the news of his release. For example, a senior member of the islamicawakening.com forum, a prominent English-language Salafi website, responded to news of his release by writing: "AllahuAkbar! AllahuAkbar! Nothing describes the happiness of the mu'mineen [faithful] all around the world this day. AllahuAkbar! Our beloved Shaykh is released!" Similarly, on islambase.co.uk, the online home of many British extremists, one member described his release as "the best news in ages." Their attitude suggests that despite the death of Zarqawi and his own long imprisonment, Maqdisi's teachings—a mixture of bigotry and pragmatism—are still seen as relevant. Indeed, Maqdisi's correct predictions in 2004 and 2005 that Zarqawi's attacks on Muslim civilians would undermine support for al-Qaeda both in Iraq and abroad may have further boosted his standing among Islamic extremists worldwide. In light of Maqdisi's influence and popularity it is worth examining his key ideas in detail.

Maqdisi on Takfir

Like many jihadis, Maqdisi's ideology depends on declaring takfir against his Muslim rivals in order to permit violence against them. However, he repeatedly says that declaring takfir should not be undertaken lightly; in his 1997 book This Is Our Aqeedah (creed), he frequently quotes Qadi Iyad, a 12th century judge from Grenada, as saying: "Declaring the blood of those who pray, who are upon tawhid [belief in the unity of God], to be permissible is a serious danger".

Maqdisi adds that takfir should only be pronounced against those who have abandoned tawhid. He says a Muslim abandons tawhid, and hence Islam, if their actions show allegiance to un-Islamic entities by aiding them or participating in their legislation. In other words, he says only those who actively support non-Islamic governments or oppose jihadis should be targeted. Unlike many al-Qaeda members,

Maqdisi repeatedly warns on both moral and strategic grounds against pronouncing takfir—and hence carrying out attacks—against ordinary Muslims, saying that in the absence of an Islamic state, it is understandable that many Muslims are unable to perfectly practice Islam.

In his July 2004 book, An Appraisal of the Fruits of Jihad (Waqafat me'a themerat al-jihad), he writes contemptuously of jihadis who "start bombing cinemas or make plans to blow up recreation grounds, sports clubs and other such places frequented by sinful Muslims." Similarly, in This is Our Aqeedah, he criticizes extremists who kill for small infractions of Islamic principles: "The shaving of the beard and imitation of the kuffar (infidel) and other forms of disobedience like it is a general affliction that is spread far and wide. It is not suitable by itself for evidence of takfir."

On Democracy

A large proportion of Maqdisi's writings are devoted to the discussion of democracy, which he regards as one of the main threats to Islam. Maqdisi does not object to democracy as a form of representative government, however, but because legislators deliberately create man-made laws to replace or supplement the sharia (Islamic law).

Maqdisi's arguments stem from his belief that a Muslim's faith is not complete unless he lives under sharia law. As he wrote in his early 1990s book, Democracy is a Religion (Al-Deemoqratiyya Deen): "Obedience in legislation is also an act of worship". Maqdisi consequently argued that anyone seeking to create legislation to replace the sharia is effectively seeking to take the place of God. From this, he concludes that "anyone who seeks to implement legislation created by someone other than Allah, is in fact a polytheist." Yet his dislike for democracy is not absolute; he accepts that consultation (shura) between a Muslim ruler and his subjects is a valid Islamic principle—but says that this principle has been hijacked by secularists to legitimize the legislative aspect of democracies. Unlike many al-Qaeda fighters, however, Maqdisi says that the illegitimacy of legislative elections does not necessarily permit attacks against anyone who votes, since some people vote only "to choose representatives for worldly living" rather than to subvert the sharia.

On Jihadi Tactics

Maqdisi believes that violent jihad against non-Muslims is a core part of Islam which can be carried out by individuals at any time or place. In an interview with al-Nida magazine in 1999, he described jihad as an "act of worship that is permissible any time". He also says that jihad is not dependent on living in an Islamist state or having a Caliph, nor is it restricted to battlefields or places of open conflict. Despite this, however, Maqdisi criticizes would-be jihadis whose enthusiasm for glory blinds them to political and religious realities. In An Appraisal of the Fruits of Jihad, he mocks the "youths moved by their zeal." He continues:

"[They] have studied neither the sharia nor reality. They have newly begun practicing the religion and have not yet rid themselves of the arrogance, pride, and tribalism of their pre-Islamic days, such that some of them even consider it shameful, cowardly, and disgraceful to be secret and discrete. Others proclaim that they are carrying automatic weapons or bombs that they roam about with in their cars here and there, showing them to this person and that person; they think it is a trivial matter to blab to everyone about how they dream and hope to kill Americans and destroy the American military bases in their lands. They then become astonished at how the enemies of Allah ask him about these things when they interrogate him, and he wonders how they knew about it?!"

Maqdisi also complains that many jihadist attacks are not carried out for strategic benefit but because such attacks are easy:

"There are other young enthusiasts who oppose us by attacking churches or killing elderly tourists, or relief agency delegates—and other such trivial targets—whereby they do not consider what will benefit the da'wah [call to religion], jihad or Islam, nor do they give preference to what will cause most injury to the enemies of Allah. Rather, their choice is only based on the easiest target."

Maqdisi describes the best mujahideen as those who are "looking for targets that will bring down the enemy combatants and defy them—such as nuclear weapons, or intelligence centers and political posts, or centers of legislation and economy in the land of the polytheists".

Maqdisi also criticizes those who attack Shiite Muslims, objecting to the attacks on both theological and practical grounds. In a 2005 interview with al-Jazeera, he said that ordinary Shiites could not be held responsible for their beliefs: "The laypeople of the Shiite are like the laypeople of the Sunna, I don't say 100 percent, but some of these laypeople only know how to pray and fast and do not know the details of the [Shiite] sect". This pragmatism does not contradict his intellectual hatred for Shiite teachings, saying in This Is Our Aqeedah: "We declare our hostility toward the path of the Rawafid [the Shiites] who hate the companions of the prophet and curse them."

Maqdisi frequently writes that hating non-Muslims is an Islamic duty. In his 1984 book, The Religion of Abraham (Millat Ibrahim), he says that this hatred "should be shown openly and declared from the outset." In An Appraisal of the Fruits of Jihad, he writes that any attacks on non-Muslims are theologically justified regardless of whether they result in any progress toward creating, or "consolidating," an Islamic state and regardless of changing political circumstances: "Any fighting done for the sake of inflicting injury upon the enemies of Allah is a righteous, legislated act, even if it brings about nothing more than inflicting this injury, angering the enemy [and] causing them harm." Simultaneously, however, he argues that for strategic reasons the mujahideen should at present concentrate their efforts on trying to establish a pure Islamic state in the Muslim world, saying that "one of the greatest tragedies of the Muslims today is that they do not have an Islamic state that establishes their religion on the earth." He also says that "the mammoth, accurately planned operations that were carried out in Washington and New York, despite their size, they do not amount to more than fighting for injury"—i.e. that they were justified only because they killed non-Muslims but had no strategic benefit. Importantly, however, he also says that if such attacks make it harder for the mujahideen to consolidate and build a true Islamic state, they should be avoided.

Through his writings which simultaneously justify both extreme violence and tactical pragmatism, Maqdisi has gained an iconic status in radical circles at a time when many jihadis—perhaps including even Osama bin Laden and Ayman al-Zawahiri—are becoming increasingly discredited. As a result, a public retraction of his more extreme views would send shockwaves through the jihadist community; on the other hand, a systematic recalibration of jihadist theory focusing attacks on Western military installations and secularists in the Arab world could reinvigorate the jihadi movement and perhaps win it new followers. Given that Jordan has reportedly forbidden Maqdisi from speaking publicly as part of the conditions of his release, it seems unlikely that his views have changed while in prison.

A poem allegedly written by Maqdisi in May 2007 tellingly describes a conversation between himself and the prison authorities in which they tell him: "Renounce [your views]; many shaykhs have... Renounce and you will be generously rewarded with material [benefits]. In return, you shall [have freedom to] speak". Maqdisi records his response as "Prison is sweeter to me ... My suffering for the sake of religion is sweet."

If Maqdisi has indeed remained loyal to his ideals, much will depend on how much freedom Jordan's government gives him to propagate his ideas; Maqdisi has consistently shown himself willing to continue promoting jihadist ideology regardless of the personal consequences.

Abu Basir & Abu Qatada

Abu Basir al-Tartusi is another prolific contemporary scholar of Syrian origin. He is a slightly more moderate Salafi ideologue who resides in London, more often criticizing past jihadi mistakes and urging caution and selective action. His tone is due in large part to the scrutiny he was put under following the 2005 London train bombings. He has provided scholarly arguments to back armed resistance to tyrannical rule (by employing jihadi tactics), also prefaced on the importance of Muslims living by the Sharia.

Abu Qatada al-Filistini, born in 1960 in the West Bank, is another example of a Palestinian-born cleric who encourages jihad against apostate rule in accordance with the Sharia and is among the most frequently cited authors in the study. His writings contend that, according to the Sharia, it is every Muslim's individual obligation to overthrow and expel any secular government from Muslim lands by bombing, sabotage, coup, or other means available to them that would advance the implementation of Sharia in that land.

These Salafi scholars play a critical but not widely observed role in the global jihadi movement. Ideology is often overlooked and is considered separate from the strategic and operational aspects of Islamist militancy. Yet, the scholars behind the jihadi movement set the framework for debates and provide direction that is by and large adhered to, or is at the least a determining factor in the planning of attacks. By better understanding their role in the movement, governments combating terrorism can attempt to intervene earlier in the radicalization process and ultimately work toward undermining their influence.

The "salafi" conflict

After the war in Iraq started, Zarqawi quickly became one of the most wanted terrorists in the world. As the leader of al-Qa'ida in Iraq, he was involved in the killing of hundreds of Iraqi civilians and the beheading of US citizen Nick Berg before being killed by an American air strike in 2006. These actions were also noticed by other radical Islamists, including Zarqawi's former mentor, Abu Muhammad al-Maqdisi. In 2004 and 2005, the latter criticized Zarqawi for his extreme use of violence. This criticism and the conflict between them that followed are the subject of several academic publicationsas is the claim that al-Maqdisi's critique was a sign of revisionism. The same is true for the arguments between the supporters of the two men and how this conflict led to the establishment of a fatwa council to "protect" jihad from faulty practices.

The division among Salafi-Jihadis in Jordan started in mid-2005 when al-Maqdisi directed an open letter entitled "Munasara wa Munasaha" (Advocating and Advising) to the leader of al-Qaeda in Iraq, Abu Musab al-Zarqawi, criticizing him for targeting Shiite and Christian civilians and accusing al-Zarqawi's organization of being infiltrated by Jordanian security. The shaykh also emphasized the importance of mujahideen leadership being in Iraqi hands.

A few weeks later, al-Zarqawi responded to al-Maqdisi's letter, arguing that the latter's criticism did not have a negative impact on him but instead sabotaged the "jihad in Iraq." These accusations caused divisions to erupt between sympathizers of both parties, a situation intensified by the recent emergence of the so-called the "Neo-Zarqawists."

Similar posts have increased noticeably in jihadi forums, indicating that the division between the "neo-Zarqawists" and the "Maqdisists" is becoming deeper and suggesting that the radical faction of Salafi-Jihadis is growing in Zarqa. Although the mainstream Salafi-Jihadis (as represented by the Maqdisists) are fighting back, the neo-Zarqawists see themselves as inheriting the legacy of Abu Musab al-Zarqawi, which may play a major role in attracting young extremists to this new faction.

Several scholars briefly acknowledge that these discussions and the subsequent rifts between Jordanian radicals after 2004 are rooted in the 1990s, though there is a lack of literature on this period. It was in the 1990s that Zarqawi, Maqdisi, and several other like-minded Jordanians are said to have formed a group known as Bay'at al-Imam, or "Fealty to the Leader."

Bay'at Al Imam

The group known as Bay'at al-Imam formed during a time of regional and national turmoil in Jordan. In the early 1990s, the Middle East witnessed the first Palestinian intifada, the American-led invasion of Iraq after the latter's occupation of Kuwait in the 1990/91 Gulf War, and renewed efforts to start an Arab-Israeli peace process in Madrid in December 1991. Meanwhile in Jordan, economic problems forced the regime to raise taxes and cut subsidies, which caused prices to rise and led to protests throughout the country.

These tensions were exacerbated by the arrival of several hundred thousand Palestinians with Jordanian citizenship who were expelled from Kuwait due to the Palestine Liberation Organization's support for the Iraqi regime during the Gulf War.

One of these Palestinian returnees was 'Isam al-Barqawi, who had adopted the name Abu Muhammad al-Maqdisi, and would eventually help found the radical Islamist group mentioned above.This turmoil caused great disillusionment among many Jordanians. Economic hardship, uncertainty about the large scale in migration of Palestinians, the ease with which the American-led coalition invaded Iraq with the help of several Arab regimes despite widespread popular opposition, and the start of a peace process with Israel caused some Jordanians to lose faith in their regime altogether.

As a result, some disillusioned men began to look for radical solutions to these problems. Consequently, a disparate number of Islamist groups with vague, but radical ideas emerged in the early 1990s and engaged in violent acts against Christians, liquor stores, nightclubs, and Jordanian officials.

This trend of radicalization was reinforced by the return of the so-called "Afghan Arabs," i.e., Arabs who had gone to Afghanistan to fight the Soviet occupation and the Afghan communist regime, but later returned to their home countries. These "Afghan Arabs" were not welcomed home by the Jordanian authorities upon their return and often ended up living in poverty, frustrated by their inability to find work. With the military experience they had gained in Afghanistan, these men made a crucial contribution to the violent groups that were set up in Jordan in the early 1990s.

One of these returning "Afghan Arabs" was Ahmad al-Khalayila, who would later be known as Abu Mus'ab al-Zarqawi. Zarqawi and Maqdisi, who had also spent time in Pakistan and Afghanistan but focused on teaching there, seem to have first met in the Pakistani city of Peshawar, in the home of fellow "Afghan Arab" Abu al-Walid al-Ansari.

It is not entirely clear what their relationship was like in Peshawar, but the two met again in Jordan after Zarqawi returned from Afghanistan and Maqdisi from Kuwait, where he had moved after leaving Peshawar. According to Maqdisi, Zarqawi was "yearning to help the unity of God and the call to God."

The two attracted a group of mostly poor, uneducated young men of both Palestinian-Jordanian and East Bank Jordanian origin, some of whom had fought in Afghanistan as well. These men seem to have followed Maqdisi because he had already written nu-merous books and articles, therefore offering precisely what they had lacked: a coherent ideology.

On the basis of al-Maqdisi's radical ideas of applying takfir (excommunication) to the regimes of the Muslim world because of their alleged unwillingness to apply shari'a in full, these men formed a group that later became known as Bay'at al-Imam. Although very little has been written about "Bay'at al-Imam," much of the existing literature that does pay attention to the group describes it in far more violent terms than is justified by the available evidence. Some simply refer to the group as a "terrorist organization."

Others label it one of many "radical jihadist groups . . . whose task was to ignite a revolutionary jihad" and that was willing to use "terrorist tactics or an "anti-monarchist jihadi underground."Some even go so far as to label it "a global Jihadist recruiting network," used by Maqdisi and Zarqawi to "coordinate the movement of Jordanian fighters in and out of Afghanistan," without offering any evidence for this argument. The members of "Bay'at al-Imam" were certainly radical, but the available evidence is far less conclusive than the idea of "Bay'at al-Imam" as a "jihadi"

The first reason "Bay'at al-Imam" cannot be described as a terrorist organization is that the group formed by Maqdisi and Zarqawi never used this name in identifying itself. Its members are said to have named their group only informally and to have referred to themselves mostly as Jama'at al-Tawhid (the Society of the Unity of God) or, especially, Jama'at al-Muwahhidin (the Society of the Upholders of the Unity of God).

As one of the group's leaders, Maqdisi was adamantly against the use of the name "Bay'at al-Imam," stating that it "is a fabricated name about us that the intelligence services have stuck on us"

The name "Bay'at al-Imam," which was later used by the Jordanian press and courts to describe the Jama'at al-Muwahiddin, was not entirely fabricated, but the name of a different group altogether. During the Gulf War, a Jordanian man called Nabil Abu Harithiyya (also known as Abu Mujahid) started a group called
 Harakat Bay'at al-Imam (the Movement of Fealty to the Leader) together with another Jordanian, Ghanim 'Abduh.

Abu Harithiyya is said to have been a friend and neighbor of Maqdisi's brother-in-law, and 'Abduh was a member of the Jordanian branch of Hizb ut-Tahrir, a radical but nonviolent pan-Islamic group with branches across the world. Together, Abu Harithiyya and 'Abduh issued several communiqués in the name of this group, which believed that the Jordanian regime was un-Islamic. 'Abduh allegedly wrote a treatise entitled Ba'yat al-Imam that argued for believers to pay allegiance to a religious leader, or imam

He showed the document to Maqdisi, who liked the idea in principle, but found it impractical. Because Abu Harithiyya was later arrested and sent to prison together with Maqdisi, Zarqawi, and other members of "Bay'at al-Imam" (i.e., Jama'at al-Muwahhidin), the intelligence services likely assumed that they all belonged to one and the same group called Bay'at al-Imam.

Given the plethora of radical groups in Jordan at the time, the lack of clarity around the name "Bay'at al-Imam," and the ideological closeness between the actual Bay'at al-Imam and Jama'at al-Muwahhidin, it is quite possible that the intelligence services themselves confused or con-flated the two groups, not being able to make heads or tails of all the different names. A second reason "Bay'at al-Imam" cannot be labeled a terrorist organization is that it was not an organization, in the sense of being a structured and organized group. In fact, "Bay'at al-Imam" seems to have been similar to the many other groups that came into existence in the early 1990s, in that it was quite informal and loosely organized.

Members of Bay'at al-Imam usually met in one another's houses,as some indi-vidual members, such as Sharif 'Abd al-Fattah (known as Abu Ashraf) and Abu al-Muntasir have confirmed. Meetings were also held in mosques in various towns throughout Jordan, such as the 'Abdullah bin 'Abbas Mosque in al-Zarqa'.

The group was so informally organized that Maqdisi did not even associate the name Jama'at al-Muwahhidin with the group's actual members in Jordan, but simply equated it with his personal religious advocacy in which he had been engaged for years, even before he came to Jordan.

A third reason to reject the labels "terrorist group" or "jihadi organization" for "Bay'at al-Imam" is that it suggests that the group was primarily or even entirely concerned with planning violent action against civilians or the Jordanian regime. While there are some indications to support this view, a closer look at the literature on the group reveals that the character of the group and the nature of its activities are not consistent or clear. Several authors mention some plans for violent attacks in which "Bay'at al-Imam" was supposedly involved, but none of the plans resulted in actual armed operations.

Moreover, their information is based on the confessions of Zarqawi and Khalid al-'Aruri, another member of "Bay'at al-Imam," to the Jordanian State Security Court (SSC) or appears to come from a former intelligence official.

Given the reputation of the Jordanian General Intelligence Department (GID) with regard to the use of torture of political prisoners to induce forced confessions that can subsequently be used in the SSC, this information is suspect. Furthermore, considering the large number of radical groups active in Jordan in the early 1990s, such plans may have been wrongly attributed to "Bay'at al-Imam."

Notwithstanding the above, "Bay'at al-Imam" was caught planning one armed attack. Many sources mention that Maqdisi, after returning from Kuwait, had brought some weapons with him that had been abandoned by the Iraqi army after it pulled out of the country, which Maqdisi himself confirmed.

In 1994, after an Israeli settler called Baruch Goldstein had murdered 29 Palestinians in the Ibrahimi Mosque in Hebron, some members of "Bay'at al-Imam" wanted to plan an attack on Israel to avenge them. It is said only two members were engaged in planning this attack, namely 'Abd al-Hadi Daghlas and Sulayman Damra (also known as Sulayman Hamza).

Maqdisi reluctantly issued a fatwa to permit this operation, stating that it was legitimate, but that he himself preferred to focus on spreading his message in Jordan. However, the plans were discovered by the Jordanian security services before the attack took place, along with the weapons that Maqdisi had smuggled out of Kuwait. As a result, the whole group was arrested and tried as "Bay'at-Imam" in 1994.

In the end, 16 men were sentenced to 15 years imprisonment for involvement in this operation. "Bay'at al-Imam" was thus only involved in one attack that we can be certain of, and it is likely this was indeed the only one.

Moreover, this one attack never materialized due to intervention by the security services. If this "terrorist group" did not engage in terrorism, with what kind of activities did it keep itself busy? Their main activities were spreading their message through missionary outreach (da'wa), as well as organizing lessons and sermons that Maqdisi gave in people's houses throughout Jordan.

Members of "Bay'at al-Imam" also copied the writings of Maqdisi and distributed them among like-minded men. On called Millat Ibrahim(The Community of Abraham), which Maqdisi wrote in 1984. In this book, Maqdisi argues that contemporary Muslim rulers show loyalty to what he refers to as "man-made laws" (qawanin wad'iyya) instead of to the shari'a, which violates the unity of God (tawhid), which should be present in all spheres of life, espe-cially legislation. He calls on Muslims to disavow (bara'a) these regimes by declaring them apostates (murtaddun).

Another book by Maqdisi that builds on this idea is Al-Dimuqratiyya Din (Democracy Is a Religion), in which he writes that democracy, because it is based on the idea that the people and their laws are the ones who decide things — not God and the shari'a, is actually a different religion. Consequently, Maqdisi asserts that those who are aware of this idea and still consciously support democracy through voting and parliamentary politics are unbelievers (kuffar).

Given the fact that the Jordanian regime had organized parliamentary elections in 1989 and 1993 — the first in decades — this was a highly topical issue, and Maqdisi's book on the subject played an important role in spreading his views among Jordanian Islamist radicals.

When the members of "Bay'at al-Imam" were put on trial, the group's message of rejecting "man-made laws" and regimes that made such laws spread to a wider audience. Members of the group consciously used the platform they were given to denounce the court, the judge, the "man-made laws" on which the justice system was based, democracy, and the Jordanian regime.

While "Bay'at al-Imam" may not have been the "jihadi" (i.e., using armed violence) or "terrorist" organization that it has been described as, the group was unapologetically radical. The way in which this radicalism should be expressed, however, was disputed among the group's members. Some, most prominently Maqdisi, argued in favor of da'wa (proselytizing), while others, including Daghlas, Damra, and possibly Zarqawi too at this point, favored a more violent approach. Moreover, they probably also disagreed over what target to attack: Israel or the Jordanian regime.

When the members of "Bay'at al-Imam" were imprisoned, they continued their da'wa activities as if nothing had changed. The aforementioned Abu al-Muntasir claims that he regularly preached on Fridays, and fellow "Bay'at al-Imam" member 'Abd al-Hadi Daghlas also gave numerous sermons in the mid-1990s that were later collected and printed.

While most of these missionary activities seem to have been directed towards the group's own members and the other prisoners, this was apparently not always the case. According to one source, for example, a prison warden once informed Zarqawi that the Jordanian interior minister was going to visit them and told him and another inmate to "try to have a nice chat (kalaman hilwan) with him to show that you have changed so that you can go home."

Zarqawi allegedly answered the warden, "We have come here to call to Islam (li-nad'u li-hadha al-din), not to go home." When a group of politicians eventually came, Zarqawi warned them "by God the Most High, to be in the ranks of Islam (fi saff al-Islam) and not to help anyone against your brothers, the upholders of the unity of God."

Being the scholar of the group, Maqdisi was greatly involved in these da'wa efforts, and went even further in his attempts to engage prison personnel. In several pieces he wrote in jail, for instance, Maqdisi describes how he tried to explain to guards why — despite their own protestations — they were not Muslims, but actually unbelievers because they worked to protect and uphold an unIslamic regime and its laws.

Maqdisi appears to portray his own position in these conversations as that of a scholar with superior knowledge. This is not just apparent from the fact that the guard in one of these debates speaks Jordanian Colloquial Arabic while Maqdisi speaks Classical Arabic, but also from his use of takfir against a warden of one of the prison's departments. The warden and Maqdisi both apparently considered each other to be unbelievers, but Maqdisi claims that his excommunication of the warden carries more authority because it is based on "much Islamic legal evidence (adilla shar'iyya kathira) that I have shown you several times," while the warden's is not.

Such nonviolent, yet confrontational behavior is bound to elicit a response from others, which is precisely what happened. Bitter debates occurred between fellow Islamist prisoners from the radical, but doctrinally different Hizb ut-Tahrir that sometimes ended with the parties accusing each other of unbelief.

One non-Islamist prisoner recalled how he came to know "Bay'at al-Imam" in prison and was shocked by their ideas, believing they would tear society apart with their willingness to brand some people who disagreed with them as infidels, and even wrote an article to warn others about them.

Prison personnel were cautious, if not hostile towards the radical members of "Bay'at al-Imam," frequently moving them from one prison to another in order to keep members apart and stop them from recruiting new followers. There were regular conflicts between the group's members and the personnel over violence against inmates and the wearing of prison uniforms. Members of "Bay'at al-Islam" are said to have protested such measures with the limited means at their disposal, which included blocking doors or refusing to follow daily routines.

While "Bay'at al-Islam"'s activities in prison were largely nonviolent, members' recollections of a particular incident perhaps illustrate the group's motivation behind their missionary activities. This incident suggests that some members of "Bay'at al-Imam" thought that they were part of a divine plan to resist the "infidel" regime inside prison. In this conflict, prison guards hurled tear gas canisters at the prisoners, leading 'Abd al-Hadi Daghlas to shout, "We have come to die!" The prisoners reportedly noticed, however, "that God honored them so that the gas thrown at them by force did not affect them."

When the inmates protesting their treatment later went to sleep, one of them had a dream about the Prophet Muhammad's army commander Khalid bin al-Walid and his companions coming to help the prisoners, telling the dreaming inmate not to worry because God would meet the requirements of the believers. When Zarqawi heard about this dream, he was delighted and considered it a sign.

Throughout its existence, "Bay'at al-Imam" had been an informally organized group, as shown above, and up until this point had not had a real leader. According to Abu al-Muntasir, however, Zarqawi and Khalid al-'Aruri argued from the time before their imprisonment that the group should have an official leader.

Abu al-Muntasir claims that they decided early on that Zarqawi would be the group's leader, while Maqdisi would be in charge of missionary activities, though it is unclear what this meant in practice. It seems obvious that a loosely organized group without a clear idea of what to do would naturally gravitate towards Maqdisi with regard to da'wa because of his seniority in knowledge and experience. When the group went to prison, its members organized, and Maqdisi is said to have then become its leader.

However, after prison guards beat a member of the group, leadership shifted from Maqdisi to Zarqawi, when the former was allegedly reluctant to take action after the incident. Although Maqdisi himself claims that he and the rest of the group successfully protested the supposed insults to Islam by the prison personnel, it is clear that the admiration he enjoyed from the group was mostly due to his knowledge, not his leadership skills. As a result, Zarqawi was made the new leader of "Bay'at al-Imam."

Maqdisi himself would later claim that he gave up leadership of the group willingly in order to focus on writing and teaching, but he would also down-play the matter by stressing he was only resigning the leadership of a small group, and not a state or anything important.

Maqdisi's account may be a correct description of what happened, due to his inclination towards da'wa. Nevertheless, it seems that the two men's reputations began to diverge from this point onward. In the few pages dedicated to "Bay'at al-Imam" in the existing secondary litera-ure, perhaps no other issue features as prominently as Zarqawi's personality. He is described in various publications as a tough man of action when he was in prison, who used makeshift weights to keep himself fit and was aggressive towards those who got in his way.

Given this toughness (ostensibly developed in Afghanistan and during his former career as a petty criminal) and loyalty to his fellow prisoners, Zarqawi seemed a natural leader in prison, where such characteristics are presumably seen as important qualities. This was also apparent in his treatment of other prisoners, whom he appears to have subjected to a strict regime, dictating what they should wear, what they should read, and when they could watch television.

Zarqawi's personality — characterized as it was by toughness, action, and discipline — contrasted sharply with that of Maqdisi. Not only was the latter a middle-class man of Palestinian origin — unlike the poor, East Bank Jordanian Zarqawi — but he was also friendly in his approach towards others, focused on reading and writing, and was perhaps more submissive in the face of violence.

Maqdisi is described as an easygoing man in prison who had normal relations with people, even those with whom he disagreed, and as someone who was very preoccupied "with knowledge", sometimes to the annoyance of others.

It is tempting to conclude from this that Maqdisi was a compromising and weak man, while Zarqawi was the exact opposite, as Abu Qudama Salih al-Hami — Zarqawi's brother-in-law and admiring biographer — has indeed concluded. Hami states that the other prisoners "considered [Maqdisi] to be opportunistic.

Although Hami's personal grudge against Maqdisi for criticizing Zarqawi means that his description of Zarqawi should be treated carefully, it seems that Maqdisi was indeed much friendlier and more tolerant than Zarqawi. Nevertheless, a Jordanian lawyer involved in the case of "Bay'at al-Imam" claims that members of the group were tortured by the General Intelligence Directorate, and several of their fellow prisoners claim that Maqdisi was one of them.

In fact, Hami himself writes that torture exacted a heavy toll from Maqdisi and that, apparently after one particularly brutal torture session, "some of his brothers did not [even] recognize him until he recognized them himself . . . and they cried over his condition."

This suggests that descriptions of Maqdisi as weak or feeble are exaggerated and that he probably could only be described as such in comparison with Zarqawi, who did seem to possess much more of the personal qualities a leader of radical Islamist inmates needs.

This became particularly clear when the members of "Bay'at al-Imam" were released as a result of the royal amnesty following King 'Abdullah II's succession to the throne in 1999. After his release, Maqdisi stayed in Jordan to continue his missionary activities, while Zarqawi, Daghlas, and several others went abroad to engage in jihad. Maqdisi has made it clear that their decision dismayed him, but also that he was not surprised, given Zarqawi's (and perhaps others') lack of patience to study and focus on da'wa

While the strict security situation in Jordan was a push factor in motivating members of "Bay'at al-Imam" to go abroad to relocate, the lure of al-Qa'ida's global jihad also acted as a pull factor for many radicals. This brings us to a final dimension of the differences between Maqdisi's and Zarqawi's leadership: jihadi authority.

While differences in personality and, to a lesser extent, ideological disagreements between Maqdisi and Zarqawi are mentioned in existing literature as a cause for their breakup, the issue of jihadi authority is entirely absent. Jihadi authority refers to the perceived status to speak authoritatively on armed jihad. One might expect Islamic scholars to have the most authority in this regard since they are experts on the religion from which jihad stems. This is true to a certain extent, and it is probably also the reason why some radical Jordanian Islamists flocked to Maqdisi in the early 1990s.

As time went by, however, it seems that the members of "Bay'at al-Imam," particularly when they were in prison, started favoring jihadi experience (i.e., having actually fought in a jihad) over religious knowledge on this subject, leading to a simultaneous devaluation of Maqdisi's status and a rise in Zarqawi's.

Though both Maqdisi and Zarqawi had gone to Afghanistan, only the latter had actually fought there, even if he came too late to fight the Soviets. The question of combat experience in a successful jihad against Afghanistan's Soviet occupiers and local communist regime became increasingly important to establishing jihadi authority among radical Islamists in general, and among members of "Bay'at al-Imam," in particular, during the group's imprisonment. Romanticizing of the Afghan jihad was not uncommon and could also be seen in Zarqawi's behavior in prison. Several authors state that he is said to have worn Afghan clothes in prison and that he took credit for his participation in battles in Afghanistan, but they only mention this in passing.

It seems, however, that such things were part of a development in which participation in the armed jihad in Afghanistan came to be seen as a quality that trumped all others in establishing jihadi authority.One former fellow inmate who was imprisoned with "Bay'at al-Imam" speaks highly of Zarqawi and several other members of the group, precisely because they fought in an actual jihad, as opposed to Maqdisi, whom he despises for not having done so, but nevertheless had the temerity to criticize Zarqawi.

Another former fellow prisoner states that, once in prison, the "Afghan Arabs" were increasingly divided into two groups: one consisting of men who had actually fought in Afghanistan and another comprised of people who had merely been there, but had not participated in combat. The former, he states, were seen as heroes, while the latter often joined them in admiration.

This is confirmed by Hami, who writes that there were "Afghan Jordanians [in prison] of whom none had [actually] gone to Afghanistan". He also stresses that the group had three leaders in prison prior to Maqdisi, at least two of whom had extensive experience in the Afghan jihad. This contrasts sharply with Maqdisi, about whom Hami keeps reminding his readers that "he was not a known fighter (muqatil) or jihad fighter (mujahid) who lived between the bullets, the missiles, and the tanks for [even] a day".

Given his lack of fighting credentials in Afghanistan, Hami claims Maqdisi knows little about jihad and does not have the authority to rule on issues in this regard. Hami states that the mujahideen perceive a reality that Maqdisi and others like him do not understand. The mujahideen, he states, acquire "knowledge of Islam through a way that is higher (asma), purer (asfa) and deeper (a'maq) than [that of] those who read and study it while they are behind their desks."

Considering such high regard for combat experience at the expense of scholarly knowledge, as well as the presence of several prisoners who had actually fought in Afghanistan, it is not surprising that having participated in the Afghan jihad became a mark of distinction for the members of "Bay'at al-Imam" and others.